W9-BTS-222

# ESTIMATION

## Penny Dowdy

# Crabtree Publishing Company

www.crabtreebooks.com

**Author**: Penny Dowdy
**Coordinating editor**: Chester Fisher
**Series editor**: Jessica Cohn
**Editors**: Reagan Miller, Molly Aloian
**Proofreader**: Crystal Sikkens
**Project coordinator**: Robert Walker
**Production coordinator**: Margaret Amy Salter
**Prepress technician**: Margaret Amy Salter
**Logo design**: Samantha Crabtree
**Cover design**: Harleen Mehta (Q2AMEDIA)
**Design**: Tarang Saggar (Q2AMEDIA)
**Project manager**: Santosh Vasudevan (Q2AMEDIA)
**Art direction**: Rahul Dhiman (Q2AMEDIA)
**Photo research**: Anju Pathak (Q2AMEDIA)

**Photographs:**
© Alamy: Lisa Ryder: p. 9
© Dreamstime: p. 10, 14 (girl), 16 (girl), 18
© Ingram photo objects: p. 16 (table)
© Jupiter Images: PolkaDotImages: p. 14
© Q2amedia: p. 1 (blocks), 4, 6, 11, 13, 14 (blocks), 15,
   16 (blocks), 17, 19, 21, 23
© Shutterstock: Andresr: p. 8; Darren Baker: p. 1 (girl),
   7 (girl); Lars Christensen: cover; Elnur: p. 5; MaxFX:
   p. 1 (background), 7 (background)

**Library and Archives Canada Cataloguing in Publication**

Dowdy, Penny
   Estimation / Penny Dowdy.

(My path to math)
Includes index.
ISBN 978-0-7787-4337-8 (bound).--ISBN 978-0-7787-4355-2 (pbk.)

   1. Estimation theory--Juvenile literature.  I. Title.
II. Series: Dowdy, Penny. My path to math.

QA276.8.D69 2008          j519.5'44          C2008-906087-3

**Library of Congress Cataloging-in-Publication Data**

Dowdy, Penny.
   Estimation / Penny Dowdy.
      p. cm. -- (My path to math)
   Includes index.
   ISBN-13: 978-0-7787-4355-2 (pbk. : alk. paper)
   ISBN-10: 0-7787-4355-1 (pbk. : alk. paper)
   ISBN-13: 978-0-7787-4337-8 (reinforced library binding : alk. paper)
   ISBN-10: 0-7787-4337-3 (reinforced library binding : alk. paper)
   1. Estimation theory--Juvenile literature.  I. Title. II. Series.

   QA276.8.D69 2008
   519.5'44--dc22

                                              2008040146

# Crabtree Publishing Company

www.crabtreebooks.com          1-800-387-7650

**Published in Canada**
**Crabtree Publishing**
616 Welland Ave.
St. Catharines, Ontario
L2M 5V6

**Published in the United States**
**Crabtree Publishing**
PMB16A
350 Fifth Ave., Suite 3308
New York, NY  10118

**Published in the United Kingdom**
**Crabtree Publishing**
White Cross Mills
High Town, Lancaster
LA1 4XS

**Published in Australia**
**Crabtree Publishing**
386 Mt. Alexander Rd.
Ascot Vale (Melbourne)
VIC 3032

# Contents

# The Contest

Sima goes to the art store. They have a sign that says, "Win Art Supplies!" Sima wants to win the **contest**.

She must guess the number of erasers in a jar. The person with the closest guess will win. Sima studies the jar. How will she guess the right number?

How many erasers do you see?

It is easy to count the pencils!

# An Estimate

Sima needs to make an **estimate**.

An estimate is a smart guess. A smart guess is something that you can really do. Try to estimate how many erasers you can hold. Look at the size of the erasers. A smart guess for many people is 10 erasers.

**Activity Box**

How many pencils could you hold in one hand? Estimate. Then check your estimate.

How many erasers
could you hold?

# Why We Estimate

Sometimes Sima knows **exact** answers. The number of people in her family is an exact answer.

Other times, Sima can only make a **reasonable** guess. How many children go to her school? That is a big number. It keeps changing, too. Her answer will be a reasonable guess.

Exactly how many people are in your family?

About how many are in your school?

# Modeling

Sima has a jar and erasers at home. She will make a **model**.

A model is a copy of something. In math, a model is a copy of a problem. Sima goes home. She puts 25 erasers in a jar. Her jar is smaller than the jar at the store. Yet making the model helps her think. The model helps Sima estimate.

Each dot stands for one eraser. Count the dots.

# Close to Right

Sima's jar holds 25 erasers with room left over. She thinks that two of her jars could fit in the store's jar. How many erasers would that be? To find out, add 25 + 25 erasers.

Two of Sima's jars would be close to, but not **equal** to, the big jar. She adds 10 more erasers. Why? She thinks that two 25s are too few. She has room left over, after all!

## Activity Box

Make five rows of five dots. **Skip count** by 5 to get 25. Then make five more rows of five dots. Skip count all the dots.

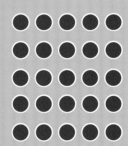

You can make dots on paper to count 25 plus 25.

Sima adds another 10.

13

# Chunking

Sima goes back to the store. She looks closely at the jar again. She looks through the top of the jar.

Sima is looking at the **chunk** of erasers at the top. How many erasers are in that chunk? One by one, Sima counts the erasers at the top.

**Activity Box**

A chunk can be any part of a thing you are estimating. It can come from the top, bottom, or side! Think of ways you can use chunks.

It would be easier to count
the chunk if it looked like this!

# Add Chunks

The chunks are on top of one another. How many layers of chunks are there? Sima looks at the side of the jar to see the layers. That way, she can estimate by **chunking**.

Decide how many erasers are in one chunk. Then decide how many chunks are in the whole group.

This is the chunk that
Sima uses in her estimate.

# More Counting

Sima counts the number of chunks in the jar. Each layer is one chunk. Each chunk has about 15 erasers.

There are six layers. So she counts to 15 six times. She uses dots on paper to help count that high. The amount she gets is 90.

**Activity Box**

How many erasers do you think are in the jar now?

Sima counts six chunks in all.

# Did Sima Win?

Sima waits for the day when they pick the winner. She has worked hard on her estimate.

Here are the three people who had the closest guesses. The person with the closest guess is the person who won.

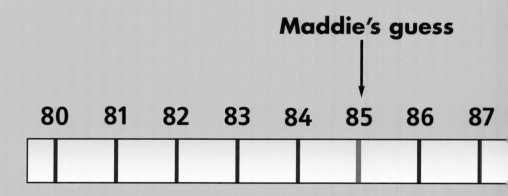

**Maddie's guess**

| 80 | 81 | 82 | 83 | 84 | 85 | 86 | 87 |

**Activity Box**

Did Sima win the contest?

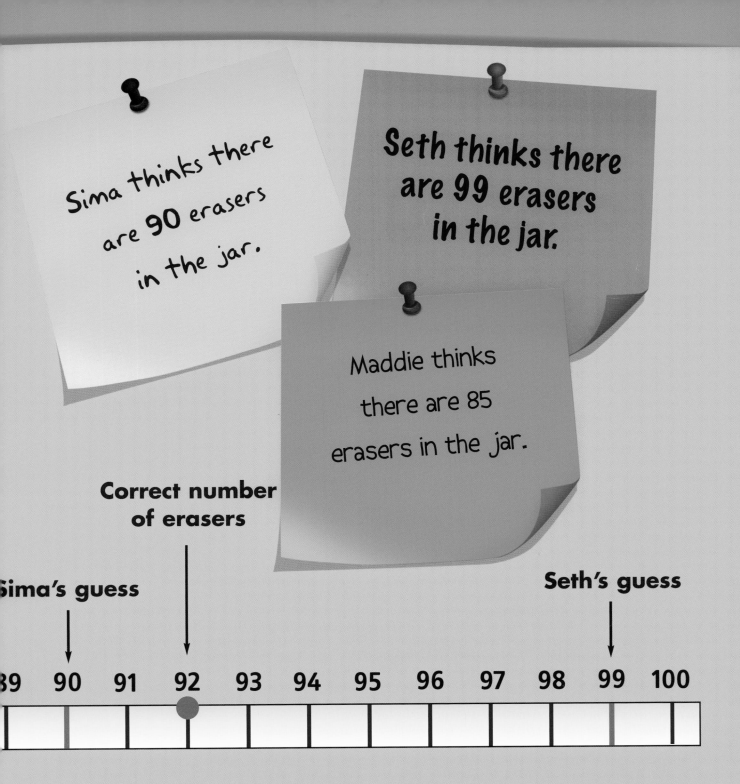

# Glossary

**chunk**  A section or a part of a group

**chunking**  Estimating by finding parts of a group

**contest**  A game or race in which there is a winner

**equal**  Two or more groups with the same amount or number

**estimate**  A smart guess or an answer close to an amount

**exact**  Precise or correct

**model**  A copy or an example of a problem shown in order

**reasonable**  Something that makes sense

**skip count**  To count by numbers other than 1

# Index

Printed in the U.S.A. — CG